Hawaiian Islands

Legend
(See Glossary on page 84)

1. Halema'uma'u
2. Kea'au
3. Hā'ena, Hawai'i
4. Pana'ewa Forest
5. Hilo Village
6. Waipi'o Valley
7. Waimanu Valley
8. Pololū Valley
9. Wailuku, Maui
10. Honolua
11. Hālawa Valley
12. Kaunakakai
13. Makapu'u
14. Mokoli'i
15. Kauhi'īmakaokalani
16. Ko'olau Mt.
17. Kahuku
18. Pōhaku-o-Kaua'i
19. Ka'ena Point
20. Ka'ala Mt.
21. Wai'anae
22. Kou (Honolulu)
23. Nu'uanu
24. Hā'ena, Kaua'i
25. Kalalau
26. Honopū

Kaua'i

Ni'ihau

O'ahu

Moloka'i

Maui

Lāna'i

Kaho'olawe

Hawai'i

Ka'ie'ie Waho Channel

Kaiwi Channel

'Alenuihāhā Channel

Puna
Kīlauea
Hilo
Hāmākua
Hāmākua
Kohala
Kona
Ka'ū

Pele and Hi'iaka
A Tale of Two Sisters
Retold and Illustrated by
Dietrich Varez

PETROGLYPH PRESS

Dedicated to the
Hawai'i Volcanoes National Park
and the
Volcano Art Center

Colorization of cover art created by The Magic Mo
www.TheMagicMo.com
www.DVarez.com

ISBN 978-0-912180-69-4

Published in Hawai'i by the
Petroglyph Press, Ltd.
160 Kamehameha Avenue - Hilo, Hawai'i 96720
Phone (808) 935-6006 - Fax (808) 935-1553
Toll Free 1-800-866-8644
PetroglyphPress@hawaiiantel.net
www.PetroglyphPress.com

First Edition
October 2011
2nd Printing - March 2014

Introduction

This book began simply as an excuse to make more blockprints. I'm always on the lookout for Hawaiian stories, myths and legends of which I can make illustrations. So, when I discovered Nathaniel Emerson's *Pele and Hi'iaka*, I couldn't resist all that potential for making more prints of such a wonderful story.

Such stories and legends long remained unheard because they were secluded in oral tradition. They had to be recorded for us to know about them. Gradually some were translated into written language and, like Emerson's writing of *Pele and Hi'iaka*, became available in English.

So another unique opportunity presented itself: the making of visualizations of the written text. I shamelessly chose to seize this opportunity to convert the oral into the visual and thereby engrave these Hawaiian cultural treasures even deeper into permanence. Who could resist such an opportunity?

Dietrich Varez
Volcano, Hawai'i

5

Pele, goddess of

Hawai'i's volcanoes, was driven out of her homeland after a quarrel with her older sister Nāmakaokaha'i. Nāmaka was a sea goddess who resented Pele's fiery nature.

Pele readied her great double-hulled voyaging canoe Honuaiākea and left Kahiki enroute to Hawai'i. She was accompanied by a number of relatives, including a shark-god brother who navigated, and her youngest sister, Hi'iakaikapoliopele, the heroine of our story.

Arriving at the northwestern-most part of Hawai'i, Pele first encountered the reefs and shoals of Mokupāpapa. Starting at Nihoa, she tested all the islands in turn to find a suitable place to settle. She dug with her legendary digging stick, pāoa, to find the fire she required.

None of the islands seemed to suit her until she reached Hawai'i, the largest island. There in the upland region of Kīlauea, she found exactly what she longed for. This would be her home. Pele settled into the fiery lava pit of Kīlauea, and our story begins there.

A wonderful place this home of Pele! Hiʻiaka, the youngest sister, was immediately charmed by it. She especially loved the scarlet lehua blossoms that were everywhere, and the flurries of red, nectar loving birds that hovered over the clustered blossoms.

One day Pele suggested to her sisters that they visit the ocean at Hāʻena in Puna to enjoy the surf and gather shellfish. The sisters all agreed. At the beach, Hiʻiaka decorated all her sisters with the scarlet lehua blossoms and then gracefully danced the hula for them.

Pele chose a cool, shady spot on a slab of lava and fell asleep. As she slept a dream came over her. She heard the music of hula pahu drums calling out to her. It was irresistible. In her spirit form, she rose from her physical sleeping body and went in pursuit of the music.

The music drew her away from the seashore at Puna and eventually brought her to the island of Kauaʻi, where a crowd was gathered at a hula performance.

8

Pele strode boldly

into the assembled onlookers. The crowd parted for the beautiful and mysterious woman in red. Side glances and whispers were exchanged as Pele made her way toward the source of the music.

There, in the midst of other performers, sat the handsome young chief named Lohiʻau, as two moʻo women in human form flirted with him. The whole company fell silent at Pele's approach. When Lohiʻau and Pele's eyes met, he was captivated by her intensity and vibrancy. Lohiʻau invited Pele to sit at his side. The dancing and feasting continued as the pair exchanged greetings and courtesies as was customary.

After the performance, Lohiʻau invited Pele to come with him and share in the hospitality of his home. After three days, she proposed to him that he come to stay with her in Puna on the island of Hawaiʻi. She would prepare a place for him and send a woman to escort him on the journey. He agreed to come, and Pele, in her spirit form, disappeared before his very eyes.

10

Lohi'au was in a daze. He wondered whether he had dreamed it all. The woman, Pele, was gone. He searched outside the house as well, but she wasn't there either. And gone with her was his spirit. He sank into a deep depression and would not come out of his house.

Eventually Lohia'u's sister, Kahuanui, and some friends, led by Lohi'au's closest companion, Paoa, dared to enter his house. Lohi'au had not been seen for days.

To their shock, they found Lohi'au dead in his home. Only his trusty dog, ever by his side, sat there by his master's lifeless body.

Paoa flew into a rage. He tore off his malo and swore an oath never to clothe himself again until he had avenged his friend's death, a traditional Hawaiian custom of mourning. He swore to hunt down Pele and make her pay for Lohi'au's death and humiliation.

Lohi'au's grief-stricken people tenderly lay his body to rest, with his faithful dog standing guard at the burial site.

12

While Paoa bewailed Lohiʻau's death on Kauaʻi, the sisters of Pele, at the seashore in Puna, had other concerns.

Pele was still asleep on her lava slab, and some of the anxious sisters thought she might be dead. She hadn't moved for days. However, none of the sisters dared to attempt waking Pele. To do so would incur serious consequences from the fiery Pele should she just be sleeping.

The sisters decided it would be best, and safest, to ask young Hiʻiakaikapoliopele to approach the sleeping Pele. Hiʻiaka, Pele's most beloved sister, was sent for. The messenger, Pāʻūopalaʻā, told her of the problem.

In her youthful innocence, Hiʻiaka shrugged off the fears of the older sisters and promptly sat at Pele's side reciting a chant, encouraging her to awake. Instantly, the roaming spirit form of Pele returned to her physical sleeping body, and the volcano goddess came to life.

14

Relieved from their concerns over Pele, the sisters all returned to their home at Kīlauea.

Pele, however, had new intentions. She needed someone to go to Kaua'i to fetch her lover, Lohi'au, and bring him to Puna. To prepare her sisters for such a request, she prepared a feast of lū'au leaves, one of Pele's favorite foods. While the leaves were being cooked, she made her request to each of the sisters. None of them would agree to undertake the mission. They all cited the many perils of such a journey and excused themselves.

Pele was left with only one alternative. The girl, Hi'iaka, would have to do it.

Hi'iaka was out surfing with her dear friend, Hōpoe, when the messenger from Pele arrived to order her to appear before Pele. Hi'iaka, with her keen sense of intuition and foresight, suspected something momentous was about to be asked of her. She readied herself to go before Pele.

Her older sisters

were not happy with Hi'iaka when the girl obediently agreed to Pele's request to escort Lohi'au. Their fear and excuses seemed even more glaring and cowardly now.

Pele laid down some strict rules for Hi'iaka to follow. The young girl was not to touch or to show any affection toward Lohi'au during the trip. Only after Pele had enjoyed the lover, Lohi'au, for five days, could Hi'iaka have him for her own. Not before, on penalty of death.

And Hi'iaka, in turn, and on the advice of her older sisters, made some requests of Pele as well. She asked to be given special spiritual powers to confront the perils along the dangerous journey. She also requested of the fiery Pele that no destruction was to come to the lehua forests she loved. Nor was Pele to harm Hōpoe, Hi'iaka's dearest friend.

Pele agreed to Hi'iaka's requests and she assigned a travelling companion, the woman, Pā'ūopala'ā, to accompany her.

18

As Hiʻiaka and her companion, Pāʻūopalaʻā, readied themselves for the trip, they paused at the plateau of Wahinekapu where Hiʻiaka, with her power of far-seeing, became aware that Lohiʻau was dead. Pele scoffed at that idea and sent them on their way.

As they neared the forest of Panaʻewa they suddenly heard the squealing of a pig.

Hiʻiaka saw a beautiful girl dressed in green. The girl, named Wahineʻōmaʻo, had prostrated herself before Hiʻiaka as a sign of respect.

She offered the piglet to Hiʻiaka, whom she mistook for Pele, and was about to make a request when Hiʻiaka corrected her.

Wahineʻōmaʻo explained that she was about to be married and was advised by her parents to first make an offering to Pele.

Hiʻiaka, with her magical powers, arranged for Pele to receive the piglet, and Wahineʻōmaʻo then joined Hiʻiaka and Pāʻūopalaʻā on their journey to fetch Lohiʻau.

20

Early the next morning, the three girls were making their way along a forest trail. There amidst the crimson lehua flowers was a group of girls gathering blossoms for a feast about to take place in their village.

Pāpūlehu, leader of the flower-gathering girls, immediately befriended Hiʻiaka. She presented Hiʻiaka with a lei and invited the trio to come to the village and join in the festivities.

As the abundant food was laid out Hiʻiaka was seated in the place of honor. However, Hiʻiaka noticed something at the feast. The girl, Pāpūlehu, although from an important family, had not acquired the good manners of polite society. She ate carelessly and scattered scraps of food about in a slovenly manner. Though this conduct deprived her of the divine protection Pele had given the other girls, Pāpūlehu decided to join Hiʻiaka's troupe. They continued through Puna, past the coastline near Hāʻena and onward toward Hilo.

22

Being familiar with the area they were travelling through, Pāpūlehu strongly urged Hiʻiaka to take another route. The trail through the forest was full of danger. It was the home of the dreaded moʻo Panaʻewa, a reptilian beast that would surely attack them.

Hiʻiaka, however, was determined to take the shorter, more dangerous route. And it wasn't long before the trouble began.

Disguised as simple tree stumps, deformed roots, clumps of bushes or mossy stones, the scaly, deceitful moʻo Panaʻewa and its legions attacked the girls from all directions. Hiʻiaka, using all her powers and strength, lashed out against the claws and fangs of the moʻo. Smeared with blood from the battle, she held her own, but the struggle did not go as well for Pāpūlehu. Without divine powers and protection, the girl was quickly consumed by the dreaded moʻo.

24

Pana'ewa, leader of the mo'o clan, had not yet joined the fight, waiting to see how the mo'o forces fared. Soon it became obvious that Hi'iaka was getting the best of them. Disguised as a kukui tree, Pana'ewa moved closer to Hi'iaka, who was at rest for the moment.

Pā'ūopala'ā, however, was not fooled. She called out a prayer to Pele for help. The prayer drifted over the crater of Halema'uma'u and caught Pele's ear. The goddess called upon a host of deities of nature - the Sun, the Moon, the Stars, Wind, Rain, Thunder, Lightning - to become Hi'iaka's allies and aid her in her quest.

Pana'ewa, still disguised as a kukui tree, was immediately enshrouded by a tangle of vines that held it fast. Pana'ewa could not move or flee. Hi'iaka watched as a torrential flood uprooted Pana'ewa and then washed the grovelling body out to sea.

26

The perils of their

path were not yet over. The girls eventually came to an abrupt precipice that ended the trail. Below raged the surf. The girls had to decide whether to take a lengthy inland detour or chance swimming the surf at the mouth of Waipi'o Valley. Pā'ūopala'ā and Wahine'ōma'o thought the swim might prove refreshing after the heated battle with Mo'o Pana'ewa.

Hi'iaka thought otherwise. She could sense the danger in the surf. To prove her point, she plucked a branch of a kī plant and held it over the edge of the precipice. The girls watched in doubt and were already removing their clothes to jump in. Suddenly a gray shape rose up from below. The water boiled in confusion, and the huge shark, Maka'ukiu, snatched the stick from Hi'iaka. Her point was proven. She gave battle and slayed the vicious shark, putting an end to another evil being.

Embarrassed by their doubt in Hi'iaka's better judgement, the girls quietly put their clothes back on. The long detour now seemed a much better choice.

The girls then passed through the area of Waipi'o and Waimanu Valleys. Hi'iaka knew this was the home of the ferocious jumping Mahiki mo'o led by Mo'olau. The bloody work of the mo'o became evident when the girls came upon two dismembered corpses by the side of the trail. Hi'iaka cursed the mo'o and utilized her medicinal powers to restore the grateful men to health, leaving them resting near Pololū. This made her further determined to rid the land of the cruel beasts.

Using her magical pā'ū skirt, she then went after Mo'olau himself, engaging in a fierce battle. Reinforced by help from the divine elements summoned by Pele herself, Hi'iaka made short work of the beastly horde of mo'o, killing and scattering them in all directions.

30

Hiʻiaka pursued the fleeing moʻo with a vengeance. She determined to exterminate them all. This led her to loop back on her trail, and after passing through Hāmākua, she and the girls soon came to the banks of the Wailuku River outside Hilo village.

Crossing that turbulent river would be a problem. There was only one way, by means of a rickety plank laid across a narrow point over the raging waters below. Two greedy sorcerers had set up a toll system there. Anyone who did not pay for crossing on their plank would be plunged off into the surging river below. All of Hilo village was held hostage to their toll. The people had no choice but to pay.

Hiʻiaka spotted these extortionists for what they were. She knew they were but more moʻo in disguise. After the exchange of a few words, Hiʻiaka set upon them and tore them apart. The village of Hilo was free again and the people rejoiced.

32

Hiʻiaka humbly accepted the thanks bestowed upon her by the people of Hilo village who were now rid of their oppressors.

At this time, the girl, Pāʻūopalaʻā, decided to leave the group and take up with a man from Kohala named Pākiʻi.

Wahineʻōmaʻo and Hiʻiaka travelled on and soon reached the famed surfing spot known as Honoliʻi. The stream there was calm and shallow as it emptied into the bay. The two girls decided to take off their clothes and held them above their heads to protect them from the adverse effect of the water as they waded across. But their nakedness was observed by a spirit who dwelt there and chided them for their immodesty. Hinahinakūikapali was the name of this spirit, and it is said that he still lives there today. Hiʻiaka in turn rebuked the spirit for spying on them.

Eventually the two girls reached Kohala where Hiʻiaka arranged for passage on a canoe headed for the island of Maui.

The seas were calm during the crossing of the 'Alenuihāhā channel to Maui. Nai'a, the porpoise, and koholā, the whale, accompanied the canoe and made occasional appearances on the surface.

But the situation aboard the canoe was not as calm and pleasant for Hi'iaka. She had reclined somewhat in the narrow confines of the small canoe. The soft breezes ruffled her pā'ū as she dozed off. This was enough to arouse the lust of the old steersman seated just behind her. He reached out for the girl just as she awoke. Exposed and discovered in his attempts, he quickly jerked back and resumed paddling. Hi'iaka was not fooled, and when the old sailor tried it a second time, Hi'iaka struck his hand away and chided him for his shameless behavior.

When the canoe finally slid smoothly ashore on the sands of Maui, Hi'iaka and Wahine'ōma'o were very glad to be free from the ill-mannered sailor.

There on Maui, at the place known as Wailuku, Hiʻiaka planned to visit her sister, Kapoʻulakīnaʻu. As the two girls approached the house where Kapo lived, they found no one at home.

Moving on around the island to the wave-battered beach at Honolua, they beheld an incredible sight. It was a girl without hands, crippled from birth, gathering shellfish at the rocky seashore. The crippled girl seemed to be having a wonderful time, dancing about in the crashing surf. As each wave receded, the girl gathered more shellfish, and as the wave came in again, she withdrew up the beach for safety.

Wahineʻōmaʻo was enchanted by the maimed girl's joyful attitude and sought to befriend her. But Hiʻiaka warned that this was not a real girl, but rather just a spirit of the real person. Wahineʻōmaʻo would have to wait to befriend the girl, Manamanaiakaluea.

With Wahine'ōma'o

looking on in amazement, Hi'iaka then promptly seized the spirit girl and bundled her up in the end of Wahine'ōma'o's garment.

Hi'iaka intuitively knew the direction of the house where they would find the real girl. As they neared the house, Wahine'ōma'o could feel the spirit becoming restless in her garment folds. The spirit wanted eagerly to reunite with the real body in the house.

At the house, Hi'iaka met the heartbroken, mourning parents of Manamanaiakaluea as they sat by the body of their dead daughter. Courtesies were exchanged, and then Hi'iaka miraculously united the spirit with the girl's real body.

Overjoyed with her new body and restored hands, the girl personally prepared food for Hi'iaka, exhibiting all the skilled manners fitting to the occasion. Hi'iaka carefully watched the girl's efforts and found nothing wanting.

From the island of Maui, Hiʻiaka and Wahineʻōmaʻo took a canoe to the island of Molokaʻi.

There, too, the beastly moʻo had terrorized the people. Two women told their sad tale to Hiʻiaka. Their husbands had been taken from them by the moʻo. The women had wasted away from hunger and lack of support. Hiʻiaka was determined to free these people from their terror.

The moʻo were on the alert as well. As Hiʻiaka and Wahineʻōmaʻo travelled through Halawa and along the steep pali, or cliff wall of the windward side, they came to a chasm. Below the cliff was the raging surf. Only a narrow plank led across the impasse.

Wahineʻōmaʻo readily tested the narrow plank, but Hiʻiaka quickly pulled her back. The plank was actually the extended tongue of the moʻo, Kīkīpua. Hiʻiaka stretched her magical pāʻū across the abyss, creating a bridge over which they safely crossed. She then slew the salivating beast as it tried to escape.

Hiʻiaka was driven

to exterminate the moʻo wherever she could find them. It is very likely due to her efforts that we are free of these wicked creatures today.

From Kaunakakai on Molokaʻi island the girls took a canoe bound for Oʻahu. And it seems that the beauty of the two girls again tempted the two men in charge of the canoe to make unwanted advances. The Kaiwi Channel crossing was short, however, and they soon landed at Makapuʻu on Oʻahu, where Hiʻiaka and her companion slipped quickly away.

Makapuʻu was an arid place. There was nothing to eat there, and the people depended on handouts from travelers. Fish was the only food to be had. Mālei, a woman relative of Hiʻiaka, lived there. She had been appointed guardian of the parrotfish and all red fish in that area. Mālei sadly confided her miserable existence to Hiʻiaka and Wahineʻōmaʻo, bemoaning the barren land with its fish bones and parched plants.

The dry bleached

bones and skeletal remains at Makapuʻu were reason enough for Hiʻiaka to want to take leave of the old woman, Mālei.

The route Hiʻiaka now took followed along the Koʻolau mountain range. Here she and her companion were pelted with squalls of rain and stormy winds. To make matters even worse, when approaching Kualoa Point the girls were set upon by Mokoliʻi, a moʻo of that area. Hiʻiaka wasted no time in dispatching the creature and turned its body into stone. The tip of its tail is the small island named after him, or Chinaman's Hat, as some now call it.

A little further on the trail Hiʻiaka encountered a distant relative, Kauhiʻīmakaokalani. He had been turned to stone long ago. Kauhi tried desperately to free himself to accompany Hiʻiaka, but could rise only to a crouching position. Today many refer to him as the Crouching Lion.

46

The important landmarks along Hiʻiaka's journey often caused her to pause and reflect in song or chant. As she travelled around Oʻahu she praised the land. At Kaipapaʻu she gazed out at Laniloa, and then passed by Lāʻie, Mālaekahana, and Kahuku. Crossing Waimea Stream and climbing the rocky bluffs she saw the Kaʻala mountain in the distance. She heard the crashing surf at Waialua. Many places were directly related to her family history or to Pele's earlier exploits.

One such place was Kaʻena, the westernmost point of Oʻahu. There Pele had earlier heard the music and drumming that led her on in seach of Lohiʻau. It has been said that Māui, the demigod, had there attempted to unite all the various islands with one pull of his giant fishhook. From Kaʻena the spirits of the dead departed into the afterworld.

Hiʻiaka and Wahineʻōmaʻo could not help but be moved by this wondrous place. They sat by the seashore at Kaʻena and sang its praises.

One of the rock formations here to which Hiʻiaka addressed her song was a huge boulder known as Pōhaku-o-Kauaʻi. Although appearing as a mere rock, the boulder was a special being, drawn up from the ocean floor by Māui's magic hook, Mānaiakalani.

Hiʻiaka asked the Pōhaku-o-Kauaʻi deity to help her build a canoe for the journey to Kauaʻi. The deity, taking the shape of an old fisherman, consented, and helped the girls build their canoe.

As the canoe was launched into the Kaʻieʻie Waho Channel and was on its way, Hiʻiaka had a premonition that all was not well with her lehua forest at home. She suspected Pele might be acting up.

But her thoughts and fears were quickly dispersed when the canoe neared the steep cliffs at Kalalau. There, high up on the cliffside, she saw the figure of Lohiʻau, in ghostly form, signalling to her.

50

Landing at Hāʻena on the island of Kauaʻi, Hiʻiaka went immediately to the house of Mālaehaʻakoa, a man of chiefly rank, renowned as being a seer. He was lame and disabled. Because he was not able to walk to the sea, his wife, Wailuanuiahoʻāno, would carry him to the shore each morning so he could fish while she attended to her kapa making. She haughtily ignored Hiʻiaka and Wahineʻōmao when they arrived at her home, for which Hiʻiaka chanted a sharp reproof.

Hiʻiaka and Wahineʻōmaʻo found Mālaehaʻakoa by the sea, lowering his triple-hooked line into the water as he chanted for good luck. Hiʻiaka responded with an incantation. The water calmed instantly, and abundant fish came to Mālaehaʻakoa. Not only that, the old man suddenly found new vigor. He discovered he could walk again, and promptly went home to prepare a feast for his benefactors.

At the feast, Mālaehaʻakoa and his wife performed a sacred hula and recited a long chant telling of the battles and adventures of Pele.

52

The next morning,

Hiʻiaka informed the grateful aliʻi fisherman why she had come.

Mālaehaʻakoa told her that Lohiʻau was long dead out of grief over the disappearance of the beautiful woman who had come to him at the hula performance. To make matters worse, two jealous moʻo women from Honopū, Kilioeikapua and Kalanamainuʻu, had fiendishly stolen Lohiʻau's body and concealed it in a secret cave high on an inaccesible hillside. Hiʻiaka recalled the vision she had seen from her canoe as she approached the island. She knew where to find Lohiʻau's corpse, and rushed to the cliff.

Hiʻiaka observed the two females blocking the entrance to the cave. She shouted a threat that caused them to flee, leaving the opening unobstructed. However, the mischievous moʻo women had spitefully removed the rickety ladder leading to the cavern. Hiʻiaka and Wahineʻōmaʻo were forced to slowly climb the cliff by hand, calling upon the Sun to slow its movement until they arrived at their goal.

54

As they reached the mouth of the cave, Hi'iaka and Wahine'ōma'o saw Lohi'au's spirit form fluttering about just as they had seen it from their canoe. Hi'iaka quickly caught the spirit before it could escape. The real body of Lohi'au lay inside the cave.

The girls carefully prepared a calabash of herbal water and set it before the body, occasionally sprinkling Lohi'au with droplets of the medicinal water while reciting prayers of healing.

While Wahine'ōma'o held onto Lohia'u's feet, Hi'iaka seized the spirit form without delay. She held it fast and, using all her healing arts, forced the resisting spirit into the dead Lohi'au. The spirit desperately tried to flee the corpse, but Hi'iaka had sealed all avenues of escape. Lohi'au's body began to make small movements. A leg twitched. The hands moved. Eyelids quivered. The lips moved as breath returned.

Hiʻiaka's prayers

for life only grew more intense. She patiently called upon all the spiritual elements with which she had been blessed. She knew that any interruption could cause failure. Slowly the young man's eyes opened and the sparkle returned.

That night, Lohiʻau's beloved sister awoke with visions of her brother, and of how he loved the sea. Looking up toward the cliff, she saw light gleaming from the cave.

Eventually, Lohiʻau rose from his bed and stood erect. He was confused at finding himself in a cave with the two girls. Hiʻiaka explained what had taken place and how she and Wahineʻōmaʻo had revived him. He was overjoyed and stretched his body and limbs for the first time.

Looking out of the mouth of the cave, they could see the ocean below. Lohiʻau longed for the sea. He suggested that they descend from the cave to the shore. Hiʻiaka and Wahineʻōmaʻo eagerly agreed, and they all climbed down on the three rainbow bridges Hiʻiaka had prepared for them.

59

As the first glimmer of dawn began to light the sky, they cleansed themselves at the seashore of the defilement of the burial cave. The salty seawater was perfect for that. Soon their bodies shone with renewed health and vigor.

Lohi'au, forgetting all cares, reached for his surfboard and ran into the breakers with sheer joy. Even the sea creatures seemed in harmony with him, and accompanied his every ride on the blue billows. Life was good again!

At the break of day, Kahuanui came out of her house and saw with disbelief that it was her brother alive and well in the surf. Filled with joy, she shouted to her husband to take his canoe and set a course for Ni'ihau to find Paoa and the other men of the village and tell them that Lohi'au was alive.

Soon the entire village was rejoicing over Lohi'au's miraculous revival. A grand celebration was in order.

Lohiʻau's sister invited all the people of the island to participate in the celebration of Lohiaʻu's rescue from the grave and in praise of Hiʻiaka's healing gifts. Paoa, Lohiʻau's dearest friend, was among those present.

And what a celebration it was! A lavish feast was prepared and the people gathered at the hālau that was the temple of Laka, a goddess of hula. Hiʻiaka respectfully invited the gods to attend, with her recital of a prayer opening the ceremony. There was a mysterious silence over the banquet while the present, but unseen, deities partook of the feast, consuming all that was set before them.

Then the hula dancing began, and the people joyfully took part. Mālaehaʻakoa explained to them that Lohiʻau would soon be leaving to meet with Pele, goddess of the volcano. Paoa was eager to accompany his friend, but Lohiʻau asked him to remain and oversee the land in his absence.

After the celebration, Hi'iaka wasted no time in readying her canoe for the channel crossing to O'ahu. The three passengers set out at once.

Two of Hi'iaka's distant relatives had taken the form of great manō, sharks, and met her canoe in mid-channel. These sea creatures, Kua and Kahole, objected to Lohi'au becoming Pele's lover. They resented Hi'iaka for bringing a mere mortal to the goddess of the volcano. A poor match, they thought. They stirred up the sea and Hi'iaka barely escaped being swallowed by a water spout.

Hi'iaka, however, did not get angry with them. She respected them as relatives, but she had greater loyalties to her sister, Pele. After a brief pursuit, Hi'iaka drove the complaining sharks from the ocean, never to return. They were forced to become land creatures, fleeing to the mountains of Wai'anae.

During her pursuit of the two monster sharks, Hi'iaka separated from her companions, arranging to meet up with them later.

Hiʻiaka eventually came to some high ground at Pōhākea in Waiʻanae, Oʻahu. From there she could use her magical vision to look in the direction of her homeland on the island of Hawaiʻi. In the foreground she saw the canoe carrying Lohiaʻu and Wahineʻōmaʻo to their prearranged rendezvous. Then, in the distance, she saw signs in the sky that all was not well.

A flush of anger and agony overcame her as she saw in the reflecting clouds what was happening there. Pele, in a fit of jealousy and mistrust, had set Hiʻiaka's lehua forest afire and had turned Hōpoe, Hiʻiaka's dearest friend, into a rocking stone formation on the seashore at Hāʻena, in Puna, despite her promise to spare them.

Hiʻiaka was heartbroken, and the seeds of revenge began to sprout in her soul and fester in her heart. She would even the score with her cruel older sister. Her time would come soon.

After reuniting with Lohi'au and Wahine'ōma'o, Hi'iaka and her companions continued on, eventually reaching the harbor of Kou, a place we now call Honolulu.

Up Nu'uanu Stream they went, to be honored guests at the home of Pele'ula, the beautiful and distinguished chiefess who ruled that area. She had long ago been a lover of Lohi'au, and she was eager, very eager, to see him again.

Relaxing after the strains of their journey, the guests were fed and entertained with a hula performance. It was all Hi'iaka could do to keep the amorous pair separated. The kissing game of kilu was being played, and Lohi'au tried his best to win so he could have his way with Pele'ula, his old girlfriend.

But it was not to be. Hi'iaka employed her supernatural skills to foil his every attempt. It seemed incredible that the great Lohi'au should fail so utterly. In defeat, Lohi'au gracefully performed the required dance to pay his debt to the winner, impressing all with his skill in hula.

Hiʻiaka did her best to swiftly remove Lohiʻau from the temptation of Peleʻula. Soon the companions were all on a canoe bound for Molokaʻi and then on to Maui. Kohala, on the island Hawaiʻi, was their final landing place. There the woman, Pāʻūopalaʻā, appeared to rejoin the group.

As they travelled on, passing through the area of Mahiki, the scene of her fierce battle with the moʻo, they came upon a stunning view of the Hāmākua coast with its cascading waterfalls. Soon they had reached the district of Hilo, from where Hiʻiaka could easily see the havoc Pele's jealousy had inflicted upon her Puna home. This betrayal freed Hiʻiaka of her pact with Pele, and she determined to have her vengeance.

Hiʻiaka sent Pāʻūopalaʻā and Wahineʻōmaʻo ahead to Kīlauea to inform Pele of their arrival. Pele was in a fit of rage and blind jealousy. She would not believe anything they said. She came forth in her fiery form and killed them both.

Hiʻiaka soon arrived at Kilauea with Lohiʻau, after passing through the forest of Panaʻewa. Pele's entire court was assembled there to observe them as Hiʻiaka braided three scarlet lehua lei. She adorned herself with one and placed the other two around the neck of Lohiʻau.

Tying the lei about Lohiʻau's neck took some doing. Hiʻiaka struggled at it, with her arms around the handsome young man's neck. Soon the effort of tying the floral strands turned into a full embrace, accompanied by unrestrained kissing for all to see. Hiʻiaka and Lohiʻau were wrapped in each other's arms and the women of the court cried out in excitement.

Pele was furious and ordered her fiery servants, among them Hiʻiaka's sisters, to destroy Lohiʻau. The servants were so smitten by him that they made halfhearted efforts at his destruction, reluctantly casting only flaming cinders upon the pair in an effort to spare them.

This disobedience

made Pele even more angry. She stripped her servants of their rank and possessions, and banished them into poverty and disgrace.

As for Lohiʻau and Hiʻiaka, there all alone at the fiery rim of the caldera, there was no hope. Hiʻiaka prepared herself to face the coming onslaught and avert the attack upon them. The flaming lake of Halemaʻumaʻu became a cauldron of fountaining fire. Lava burst out at Keaʻau backing up into ʻŌlaʻa and splitting into two streams, one moving toward Hilo and the other continuing into Kaʻū. The fire of Pele encircled them on all sides. Pele herself had taken charge of Lohiʻau's destruction. The young man, in full delirium from the sulphur fumes and heat, offered some prayers at Hiʻiaka's request, but his fate was sealed. Pele drew ever closer, and only moments remained. Hiʻiaka's divine body could not be destroyed, but Lohiʻau's human body was consumed by lava. Pele's jealous revenge was complete.

Pele buried Lohiʻau in her lava to a depth where no one could find him. Hiʻiaka, with her supernatural powers, urgently dug down through many layers trying to unearth him.

As she dug she came upon the lifeless bodies of her loyal traveling companions, Wahineʻōmaʻo and Pāʻūopalaʻā and restored them to life.

The great god, Kāne, speaking through Wahineʻōmaʻo, implored Hiʻiaka to refrain from digging deep enough to flood Pele's domain in water, thereby throwing the whole land into chaos. Hiʻiaka's efforts to unearth Lohiʻau had failed. She finally had to let go.

Buried there under layers of lava rock, Lohiʻau's physical body was dead, but his spirit managed to free itself and it sought out his old friend Paoa, on Kauaʻi.

Paoa dreamed that Lohiʻau's spirit approached him and asked for help. Paoa's response was immediate and clear. He set out to retrieve his friend, Lohiʻau, from Kīlauea.

Paoa, who had sworn an oath in grief not to clothe himself until he had dealt revenge upon Pele for the death of his friend, entered his canoe for the journey to Hawai'i. As if of its own accord the canoe skimmed over the water and arrived that same morning at Waipi'o Valley. Paoa saw a new land and many wondrous sights as he travelled across the island of Hawai'i. He soon arrived at the steaming caldera of Kilauea.

The spirit form of Lohi'au had led Paoa throughout his travels through unfamiliar lands and finally to a rock formation nearby. Paoa immediately recognized what he confronted. He broke down in despair as he realized this was the lava-encased body of his dear friend, Lohi'au.

Hi'iaka, returning from her search for Lohi'au's body, also heard Paoa's cries and lamentations as she approached the dire scene.

Meanwhile, Pele had retreated to a cave where Paoa could not see her, but where she could hear his wailing and see his grieving form. The handsome, and unclothed, young man aroused her curiosity, and she soon called for him to be brought to her.

In the course of their conversation, Pele was captivated by Paoa's loyalty and devotion to his friend. She could not resist this handsome and brave man. As a result, Paoa soon forgot his oath of revenge. Pele's beauty and charm completely disarmed him. He spent three nights with the fiery goddess before returning to Kaua'i.

In front of Pele, Paoa had explained about his friend, Lohi'au, and how Hi'iaka had restored him to life at Hā'ena on Kaua'i. When Pele heard his words she was astonished. Hi'iaka confirmed the events and defiantly told Pele that, until the destruction of her beloved Hōpoe, there had been no exchange of affection between her and Lohi'au.

Pele, regretting her impulsive actions, apologized for her cruel deeds. All was forgiven by Hiʻiaka, but she resolved in grief to leave Kīlauea and return to Kauaʻi, accompanied by her loyal servants.

On the way, she decided to stop on Oʻahu to rest and once again visit her old friend, Peleʻula, with whom she had played kilu. There, amidst the reunion of old friends and new entertainment, Hiʻiaka suddenly heard a familiar voice joining in her chant. She could not believe her ears. Seeking out the chanter, she finally saw who it was. Lohiʻau!

It was Lohiʻau. He had been restored to life by the divine intervention of Kānemilohai, a powerful elder brother of Pele, who had reunited the young man's body and spirit.

Hiʻiaka and Lohiʻau's reunion was joyous beyond all imagination. Fate and the work of the gods themselves had brought them together again.

And that is the end of our story. It is finished. The end. Pau.

Glossary of Hawaiian Words and Names

'Alenuihāhā – Channel between Maui and the island of Hawai'i
ali'i – Hawaiian chiefly class
Hā'ena – Coastal area on the island of Hawai'i; land section, village on Kaua'i
hālau – Meeting house for hula; canoe shed
Hālawa Valley – Valley on Moloka'i
Halema'uma'u – Crater of Kīlauea volcano
Hāmākua – Land section on the northeastern side of the island of Hawai'i
Hawai'i – Largest island in the Hawaiian Chain
Hi'iaka – Youngest sister of Pele, volcano goddess
Hilo – District, land section and village on the island of Hawai'i
Hinahinakūikapali – Spiritual deity at Honoli'i on the island of Hawai'i
Honoli'i – Famed surfing spot north of Hilo on the island of Hawai'i
Honolua – Surfing and fishing area on Maui
Honopū – Remote valley on the northwest coast of Kaua'i
Honuaiākea – Name of Pele's voyaging canoe
Hōpoe – Hi'iaka's best friend
hula – The Hawaiian dance form
Ka'ala – Mountain, highest point on O'ahu
Ka'ena – Land section and point on O'ahu
Kahiki – Mythical homeland of Pele and her family
Kahuanui – Lohi'au's sister
Kahuku – Northernmost point and beach on O'ahu
Ka'ie'ie Waho Channel – Channel between Kauai'i and O'ahu
Kaipapa'u – Land section and point on eastern O'ahu
Kaiwi Channel – Channel between Moloka'i and O'ahu
Kalalau – Land section and valley on Kaua'i
Kalanamainu'u – One of two mo'o women of Kaua'i
Kāne – One of the four great Hawaiian gods of old
Kānemilohai – Elder brother of Pele
kapa – Tapa, traditional Hawaiian clothing made from tree bark
Kapo – A sister of Pele and Hi'iaka
Ka'ū – District on the island of Hawai'i
Kaua'i – Island in Hawaiian chain
Kauhi'īmakaokalani – Crouching Lion, geologic feature on O'ahu
Kaunakakai – Principal village on Moloka'i
Kea'au – Land section in Puna on the island of Hawai'i
kī – Woody plant in the lily family, also known as tī, sacred to Pele
Kīkīpua – Mo'o on Moloka'i
Kīlauea – Currently active volcano and land section on the island of Hawai'i
Kilioeikapua – One of two mo'o women of Kaua'i
kilu – A kissing game similar to spin-the-bottle
Kohala – District, land section on the island of Hawai'i
koholā – whale, humpback
Ko'olau – Land section and mountain range on O'ahu
Kou – Old name for Honolulu Harbor and nearby village
Kualoa – Land section and point on O'ahu, considered sacred
kukui – Candlenut tree
Lā'ie – Land section, bay and point on eastern O'ahu

Laniloa - Land leading to Lāʻie Point, Oʻahu
lehua - Blossom of the ʻōhiʻa tree
Lohiʻau - Pele's sweetheart and dream lover, lover of Hiʻiaka
lūʻau - Young edible leaves of the kalo (taro) plant
Mahiki - Land section in Waimea on the island of Hawaiʻi; a group of moʻo
Makapuʻu - Easternmost point and land section on Oʻahu
Makaʻukiu - Shark god that preyed on people at Waipiʻo Valley
Mālaehaʻakoa - A lame chiefly fisherman on Kauaʻi
Mālaehahana - Land division and stream on Oʻahu
Mālei - Dwells at Makapuʻu, guardian of the parrotfish
malo - Hawaiian loincloth for men
Manamanaiakaluea - A crippled girl without hands
Maui - Island in the Hawaiian Chain
Māui - Folklore hero and mythological demigod
Mokoliʻi - A small island off Oʻahu, named for a legendary moʻo
Mokupāpapa - Low reef islands located in the Northwestern Hawaiian Islands
Molokaʻi - Island in the Hawaiian Chain
moʻo - Mythical reptilian beings
Moʻolau - A leader of Mahiki moʻo
naiʻa - Porpoise or dolphin
Nāmakaokahaʻi - Sea goddess and sister of Pele
Nihoa - Highest island between Kauaʻi and Midway
Niʻihau - Island in the Hawaiian Chain
Nuʻuanu - Stream and valley on Oʻahu
Oʻahu - Most populous Hawaiian island
ʻOlaʻa - Land division in Puna on the island of Hawaiʻi
pahu - Hula drum
Pākiʻi - Male character, friend of Pāʻūopalaʻā
pali - Cliff, steep hill
Panaʻewa - Land section and forest near Hilo; leader of moʻo
pāoa - Pele's mythical digging stick
Paoa - Lohiʻau's best friend
Pāpūlehu - Traveling companion of Hiʻiaka
pāʻū - Women's skirt or sarong
pau - Finished, at the end
Pāʻūopalaʻā (Pāʻūopalaʻe / Pāʻūopalai) - Traveling companion of Hiʻiaka
Pele - Goddess of Hawaiʻi's volcanoes
Peleʻula - Female friend of Hiʻiaka, chiefess on Oʻahu
Pōhākea - Mountain pass on Oʻahu
Pōhaku-o-Kauaʻi - Legendary stone on Oʻahu
Pololū - Land section and valley in Kohala on the island of Hawaiʻi
Puna - District, land section on the island of Hawaiʻi
Wahinekapu - A bluff near Kīlauea, island of Hawaiʻi
Wahineʻōmaʻo - Traveling companion of Hiʻiaka
Waiʻanae - Land section and mountain range on Oʻahu
Wailuanuiahoʻāno - Wife of Mālaehaʻakoa
Wailuku - River near Hilo on the island of Hawaiʻi; land section on Maui
Waimanu - Valley on the island of Hawaiʻi
Waipiʻo - Valley on the island of Hawaiʻi

Publisher's Note

It is an honor and a pleasure to work with Dietrich Varez on his re-telling of the ancient Hawaiian myth of Pele and Hi'iaka, through the compelling vision of his iconic block print art. Our intention is to bring a complex story to new readers through a simplified text and a sensitive visual interpretation that honors the rich mythology passed through Hawaiian oral tradition.

There were many versions of this classic, epic tale. One of the earliest English translations, *Pele and Hi'iaka, A Myth from Hawai'i*, was authored by Nathaniel Bright Emerson and first published in March of 1915. After remaining out of print for many years it is again in print through the Edith Kanaka'ole Foundation. This book was the primary source of inspiration for Varez, who started working on this project in 2006.

Important references consulted for place and character names were: *Place Names of Hawai'i*, the *Hawaiian Dictionary*, *Hawaiian Mythology*, and *Holo Mai Pele*. *'Olelo No'eau, Hawaiian Proverbs and Poetical Sayings*, which features artwork by Varez, was also a valuable aid in the orthography.

We gratefully acknowledge the contributions of Maile Yamanaka, John R. K. Clark and Puakea Nogelmeier in sharing their mana'o. Alexander Reed gave valuable assistance in final proofreading and editing. A new vision of an ancient story will now be shared.
Christine Reed, editor

Pau

Dietrich Varez

finds inspiration for his art from Hawaiian folklore and the natural beauty of the native 'ōhi'a forest surrounding his home in Volcano, Hawai'i. His original prints are each individually created, hand-cut and produced by the artist himself in his own matchless style. A prolific and unconventional printmaker, Varez believes in making his art available to a broad, popular audience, by pricing his work so anyone can afford a hand printed, signed piece of art. Although he has had no formal art training, he has been creating his unique form of block prints since moving to Volcano and finding rich inspiration in the realm of Pele. Varez is further exploring his creativity with full color paintings in oil. His work is available at the Volcano Art Center, Honolulu Museum of Art, Bishop Museum and Kōke'e Museum. Look for his signature artwork in the Reyn Spooner line of Hawaiian clothing. Visit www.DVarez.com for biographical information and a broad selection of Dietrich's artwork.

Dietrich Varez was born in Berlin, Germany in 1939. He has made his home in Hawai'i since the age of eight, when his mother, Ursula married Manuel Varez, an American soldier who adopted her two sons and brought the family home to Hawai'i. Growing up island style on O'ahu, he attended the University of Hawai'i at Mānoa, earning a Masters degree in English. It was there he met his wife, Linda, a fellow artist, before moving the family to Hawai'i Island in 1968.

HINA, The Goddess by Dietrich Varez is also published by the Petroglyph Press.

Books published by the Petroglyph Press

A Concise History of the Hawaiian Islands
by Dr. Phil K. Barnes
Hilo Legends
by Frances Reed
HINA - The Goddess
by Dietrich Varez
How to Use Hawaiian Fruit
by Agnes Alexander
'Iwa, The Hawaiian Legend
by Dietrich Varez
Joys of Hawaiian Cooking
by Martin & Judy Beeman
The Kahuna
by Likeke R. McBride
Kona Legends
by Eliza D. Maguire
Leaves from a Grass House
by Don Blanding
Paradise Loot
by Don Blanding
Pele and Hi'iaka, A Tale of Two Sisters
by Dietrich Varez
Petroglyphs of Hawai'i
by Likeke R. McBride
Plants of Hawai'i, How to Grow Them
by Fortunato Teho
Practical Folk Medicne of Hawai'i
by Likeke R. McBride
Stars Over Hawai'i
by Edwin H. Bryan, Jr. & Richard Crowe, Ph.D.
The Story of Lauhala
by Edna W. Stall
Tropical Organic Gardening - Hawaiian Style
by Richard L. Stevens